VIRGO
August 23–September 22

If everything
was perfect,
you would
never learn
and you would
never grow.

✧ Beyoncé ✧

BUTTERCUP

Virgo

I love myself as I am

summer

Image by Andrea Lauren © Simon & Schuster, Inc.

If You Want
It Done Right
Hire a Virgo

Virgo

Ruled by Mercury

INTELLIGENT

Honest

Industrious

THOUGHTFUL

ADAPTABLE

RULING HOUSE

6

The House of Health & Work

VIRGO

✧

I respect my worth and my impact

✧✧✧

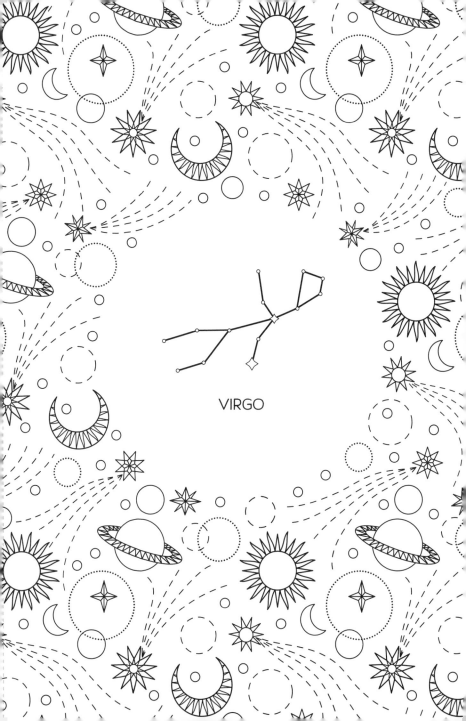

VIRGO

Aries

Taurus

Gemini

Cancer

Leo

Virgo

Libra

Scorpio

Sagittarius

Capricorn

Aquarius

Pisces

Earth Signs

Taurus

Virgo

Capricorn

LET THE STARS LEAD THE WAY